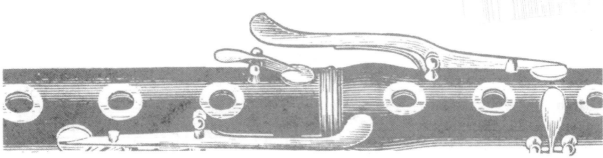

George Frideric Handel

SEVEN SONATAS

for Flute and Piano

Realization of the Figured Bass by Louis Moyse

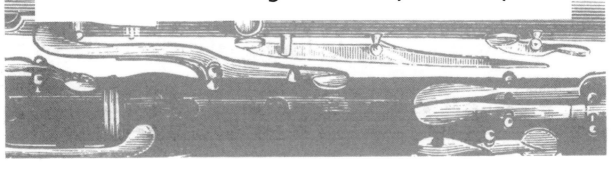

G. SCHIRMER, Inc.

DISTRIBUTED BY

HAL•LEONARD®
7777 W. BLUEMOUND RD. P.O. BOX 13819 MILWAUKEE, WI 53213

CONTENTS

45300

Sonata I

Figured bass realized by
Louis Moyse

George Frideric Handel
(1685-1759)

* The dotted rhythm should be exaggerated; the short notes should be played lightly.

** Dots and dashes under a slur indicate note should be tongued.

*** Trills start on the beat and on the higher note.

6

Adagio

attacca

Allegro

Sonata II

George Frideric Handel

Figured bass realized by
Louis Moyse

Larghetto

attacca

Sonata III

Figured bass realized by
Louis Moyse

George Frideric Handel

Larghetto

(ritmo ostinato)

Sonata IV

Figured bass realized by
Louis Moyse

George Frideric Handel

Adagio

attacca

45300

28

* Handel urtext:

45300

attacca

Bourrée

Minuetto

Sonata V

Figured bass realized by
Louis Moyse

George Frideric Handel

45300

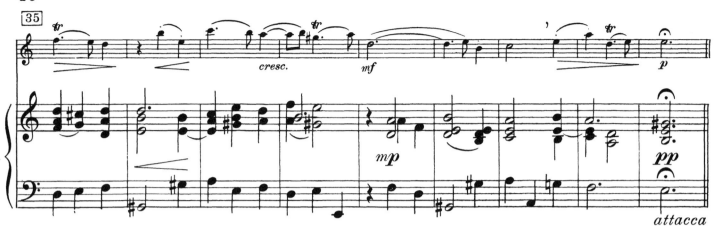

attacca

A tempo di Gavotta

Sonata VI

Figured bass realized by
Louis Moyse

George Frideric Handel

Largo

45300

A tempo di Minuetto (in 6)

Sonata VII

Figured bass realized by
Louis Moyse

George Frideric Handel

Larghetto

Siciliana

attacca

Allegro

* The bracketed two bars are not in the Urtext. They have been inserted by the editor, who feels they are necessary for a balanced ending of the movement.

Sonata I

Flute

George Frideric Handel
(1685-1759)

* The dotted rhythm should be exaggerated; the short notes should be played lightly.

** Dots and dashes under a slur indicate note should be tongued.

*** Trills start on the beat and on the higher note.

45300Cx

Printed in the U. S. A.

Flute

Flute

3

Sonata II

Flute

George Frideric Handel

Sonata III

Flute

George Frideric Handel

Flute

Flute

Sonata IV

Flute

George Frideric Handel

Flute

(Handel urtext)

45300

Flute

Sonata V

George Frideric Handel

Flute

Flute

45300

Sonata VI

Flute

George Frideric Handel

Flute

Flute

Sonata VII

Flute

George Frideric Handel

45300

22

Flute

45300

Flute

* The bracketed two bars are not in the Urtext. They have been inserted by the editor, who feels they are necessary for a balanced ending of the movement.

45300